HARTLEPOOL

THROUGH THE AGES

Paul Chrystal
& Stan Laundon

AMBERLEY PUBLISHING

To Doreen Richardson

Front cover: Two views from the top of Christ Church Tower, one from the 1950s, the other 2014. There's a policemen down there to the right of Binns, directing traffic.

First published 2014

Amberley Publishing
The Hill, Stroud, Gloucestershire, GL5 4EP
www.amberley-books.com

Copyright © Paul Chrystal & Stan Laundon, 2014

The right of Paul Chrystal & Stan Laundon to be identified as the Authors of this work has been asserted in accordance with the Copyrights, Designs and Patents Act 1988.

ISBN 978 1 4456 4044 0 (print)
ISBN 978 1 4456 4077 8 (ebook)

British Library Cataloguing in Publication Data.
A catalogue record for this book is available from the British Library.

Typesetting by Amberley Publishing.
Printed in Great Britain.

INTRODUCTION

My earlier book, *Hartlepool Through Time*, was published in 2011; its popularity prompted the publishers and I to consider a further volume. Here is that further volume, produced this time with Stan Laundon. Stan not only provides many of the old images but has taken care of the modern photography and, in so doing, has given us some stunning images of Hartlepool as it is today.

Hartlepool Through the Ages offers a further 200 or so pictures, none of which appeared in the earlier volume. All the photography is completely original, as is the accompanying text. As before, we cover the three towns that make up 'Hartlepool': 'Old Hartlepool', West Hartlepool and Hartlepool; outlying villages are again included: Greatham, Elwick, Hart and Seaton Carew, with the addition this time of Wolviston, Blackhall and Crimdon.

In a book on the history of Hartlepool, you would expect to read about that monkey, Andy Capp, and the bombardment; their virtual absence is due entirely to the fact that that all of these and many other topics are covered in *Hartlepool Through Time*. In this selection, though, you will meet Chick Henderson, Joe Brown, Terry Bell, Henry Smith, Capt. Perry, *Egbert* the tank, Compton Mackenzie, Winston Churchill and Miss Great Britain, among others. We will take you to the steelworks north and south, to Blackhall Rocks, Steetley Magnesite, Greatham Co-op and to the top of Christ Church; we will show you parts of the town by night and by day; we'll show you how to street dance on the pier and we'll watch a rehearsal of the Wizard of Oz. Altogether, *Hartlepool Through the Ages* is a warm and colourful celebration of a warm and colourful town – past and present.

ABOUT THE AUTHOR

Paul Chrystal has worked in medical publishing for thirty-five years but now combines this with writing features for national newspapers, as well as appearing regularly on BBC local radio and on the BBC World Service. He is the author of thirty or so books on a wide range of subjects, including *Hartlepool Through Time*; *Lifeboat Stations of the North East* (which includes Hartlepool and Seaton Carew); *Redcar, Marske & Saltburn Through Time;* and *The North York Moors Through Time.* He is married with three children and lives in York... although he did spend his formative years in Hartlepool. paul.chrystal@btinternet.com.

Stan Laundon was a presenter and producer on BBC local radio on Teesside for many years. He was a part of the entertainment industry during the sixties, working with pop singer Joe Brown, as well as being a columnist for the magazines *Beat Instrumental* and *Beat Monthly*. He also worked as a journalist for the *Express & Independent* group of newspapers in East London.

Stan insists that his main claim to fame is that he was the first ever disc jockey in the UK to play Chris Rea on the radio. He was involved in charity work for the Guide Dogs for the Blind, Hartlepool & District Hospice and the RNLI in Hartlepool. For information on Hartlepool's history, news and information about the town, and some stunning photography go to Stan's fascinating website www.stanlaundon.com. Stan lives in Hartlepool.

West Hartlepool Improvement Commissioners, 1870
If you ever wondered why Hartlepool is as it is, then these would have been the gentlemen to ask. They are the West Hartlepool Improvement Commissioners, posing in 1870 with Ralph Ward Jackson right in the middle there. *The Comprehensive Gazetteer of England and Wales, 1894/95* tells us that, 'The town was first governed by a board of Improvement Commissioners, established in 1854; in 1870, under the West Hartlepool Extension and Improvement Act, the boundaries were enlarged. In the jubilee year, 1887, a charter of incorporation was granted under the Municipal Act of 1882, and it is now governed by a mayor, 6 aldermen, and 18 councillors. The borough [...] has a population of 42,710'.

CHAPTER 1
Old Hartlepool

Carnival

Two shots of Hartlepool Carnival on the Headland – the first in the 1950s, the second an altogether more dramatic and colourful event in 2013. The characters are, from left to right: June Stoddart, Phyllis Wanley, Ana Faint, Roslyn Wanley; the young boy is Keith Faint, with an unknown at the end. The lady at the back, in the centre, is Ana Faint, mother of Ana and Keith. On the previous page, we have an intriguing aerial view of Hartlepool taken in 1947 and a fine picture of St Hilda's from 2014 complete with rainbow.

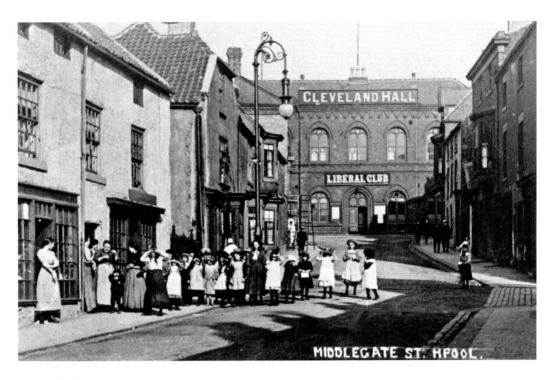

Middlegate
With the Cleveland Hall and Liberal Club on Durham Street. The Cosmopolitan Hotel is nearby, run by Kit Measor for twenty-three years. Kit not only served in the Boer War, he also played for Hartlepool Rovers.

The Old Pier

A busy day on the old pier in the 1940s with fishermen loading pots. The door of the joiner's shop is open and a door to the blacksmith's can be seen on the right. A night-time shot of nearby St Hilda's forms the newer picture.

Bowling, Putting and Tennis

Overlooked by houses in Olive Street and Marine Crescent. On 8 June 2011, the bowling green hit the national headlines when an off-course Asian robin paid an unscheduled visit, attracting 200 or so twitchers from around the country. The breed had only been seen twice before in the British Isles: on the Isle of Man in 1983 and on Skomer Island, off the south-west coast of Wales, in 1990. The bird was ringed by the The Tees Ringing Group; it has yet to make a return. The second picture is of a tennis match in action on the Town Moor in the 1950s.

CLEVELAND Rd HARTLEPOOL DEC: 1914.

Bombardment: Churchill in His Bath at the Admiralty

According to a new book by Taylor Downing entitled *Secret Warriors: Key Scientists, Code-breakers and Propagandists of the Great War* (2014), the First Lord of the Admiralty was having a bath when news was given to him about the bombardment of the Hartlepools. Churchill leapt out, realising that Admiral Sir John Jellicoe, commander of the Grand Fleet, was in a perfect position to ambush the raiders. Unfortunately, fog intervened and allowed the German battle cruisers to sail right past Jellicoe's squadron unscathed. Despite howls of protest from the British press ('where was our Navy?'), the Admiralty could not respond for fear of divulging the top secret that we had decrypted the Germans' codes and were able to read all of their signals – intelligence that had allowed Jellicoe to be where he was in the first place.

OFFICERS & MEN IN CHARGE OF HARTLEPOOL BATTERIES

The Town Wall

Two wonderful pictures of the Town Wall, separated by 100 years or so. The walls were built in the fourteenth century to defend the landward western side of the peninsula and the beach on the south side. This fortified the harbour and made Hartlepool one of the most heavily defended port towns in Britain, and the only walled town not to have a castle. The wall had three gates: one on the road to Hart, Northgate, which protected the main route into town; Watergate gave access to the harbour; Sandwell Gate, the only one to survive, provided access from the Fish Sands through the south wall. Three further gates were added later.

The Steetley Chimney
A bleak industrial shot of the Steetley chimney from Middleton Road. The modern shot shows it during demolition. As Stan Laundon describes on his website 'Just after 11.00 a.m. on Sunday, July 29th 2012 local man Dave Fricker and his grandson, Jamie Browne, won a competition to push the plunger to blast the chimney into history. Thousands of people gathered in the area to witness the demolition.'

A Bar Bar None

I've been in a few bars in my time, and many would say that a bar is a bar anywhere (except in York where, oddly, a bar is a gate) – but this is obviously not the case. The bar of The Harbour of Refuge is truly exceptional, as you can see here. The other shot shows The Harbour in the background. Built in 1895, it was preceded by a beerhouse-cum-grocers. It is known as The Pot House on account of the glazed pottery tiles on the outside walls.

13

HENRY SMITH'S SCHOOL HARTLEPOOL

Mr Henry Smith, or 'Dog' Smith
A picture of the striking effigy of Henry Smith (born 1548) from the chancel at All Saints Wandsworth where he is buried; he is in the act of devotion dressed in an alderman's gown. Henry Smith was a salt merchant by trade, a successful businessman who acquired land all over England and set up a number of charitable trusts for the relief of the poor. He died in 1628, leaving £2,000 to his trustees. Hartlepool was one of the beneficiaries. A sum of £1,000 was set aside to pay ransoms for those captured by Turkish pirates. Today, the charity make 'grants totalling approximately £25 million each year to up to 1,000 organisations and charities throughout the UK for initiatives and projects that address social inequality and economic disadvantage'. Henry Smith's School is in the other picture; it was demolished in 1982. Henry picked up the nickname 'Dog' after he apparently reduced himself to penury and attracted the attentions of a dog, who persistently followed him round.

Hartlepool's Hospital

Hartlepool's Hospital, or St Hilda's, was a wonderful old building that was sadly demolished many years ago. The old Friarage Manor House, which was part of the inside of the hospital and built in 1605, still stands on the Friarage Field and is a Grade II listed building. The top picture shows Christmastime on the children's ward around 1925. The patient next to the Sister on the left is Harry Waller, who spent six months in that bed due to an accident with his leg. Fifty years later, his daughter, Margaret Hodgman, gave birth to a son in exactly the same bed in the same ward.

The Old Ferry

A fine shot of the old ferry from Alfred Price Photographs (1890–1912), part of his original collection, which was exhibited in the Abbey Street Tea Rooms in old Hartlepool in September 2002. The collection was found in a skip. The new photograph shows The *Cygnus Alpha* setting sail on 13 May 2014, with a little help and assistance from the tugs *The Fiery Cross* and *The Phoenix Cross* at the bow with *The Svitzer Castle* and *The Ormesby Cross* at the stern and barge *UR1*. Every platform built at the Heerema Fabrication Quay has a monkey hanging from the superstructure to remind customers where it was built.

The Whale Jawbone

The jawbone and a vertebrae of a baleen whale netted off Hartlepool in the early 1930s. The sailor on the left is Frederick Arthur Abigail, who was a mate or third hand on a number of Hartlepool trawlers; he is the fifteen-year-old third from the left in the main photograph. Frederick was on minesweepers during the Second World War and shot down an attacking German fighter in 1940; he was awarded the DSM. The new picture shows the jaws of a sperm whale on the Fish Quay in 2012.

NORTHGATE, HARTLEPOOL.

No. 18 Northgate and a Water Famine

The photographer is the focus of attention in the colour photograph. The other gives a vivid picture of the 1907 water shortage with townsfolk bringing their jugs and pails to replenish their water supply. From left to right, you can see the corner of St Hilda's Hall, Church Close School, the Morison Hall, St Hilda's Vicarage. On the right is part of the St Hilda's church wall.

HARTLEPOOL WATER FAMINE APRIL 14TH 1907.

PHOTO CARTER.

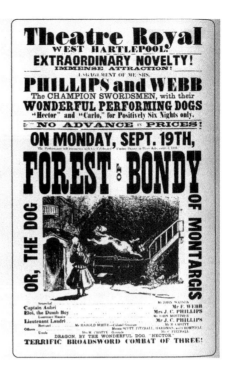

Swordfighting or Street Dancing?

A skipping rope dance by Miss Lizzie Green; broadsword combat; canine drama, performing dogs – all for the delectation of Hartlepool audiences in the mid-nineteenth century. Street dancing on a pier is your entertainment of choice for the twenty-first century – but, as Stan Laundon advises, do not try this at home.

Old Hartlepool Railway Station

Celebrations at old Hartlepool station, in Northgate, on 2 September 1956. Vic Smith provided the background relating to this photograph. He says, 'Locomotive 61443 is taking water whilst working the Stephenson Locomotive Society & Manchester Locomotive Society's "Tees-Tyne" railtour'. For more information, be sure to visit the Six Bells Junction website. It is a rare photograph of the station from the collection of local man Tony Pearson, as is the second photograph of West Hartlepool sheds in Mainsforth Terrace just before closure in 1967. The Standard Class 8F WD *Austerity* 2-8-0 number 90074 is the train in the centre.

Coal Staithes and Engine House

The old Throston Engine House, in Cemetery Road, dates back to 1830. The steam-powered hauling engine drew coal wagons up a railway incline to the top of the former coal staithes. It was a dispute between railway companies over use of these coal-shipping facilities that became a major factor leading to the founding of the new town of West Hartlepool in the 1840s. The railway wagons used to roll across the old Throston Bridge as shown on the next page.

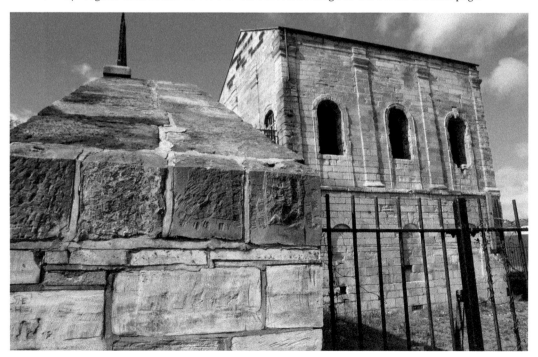

Throston Bridge

A goods train trundling over Throston Bridge on its way to the coal staithes. This was also the main route to Hartlepool railway station in Northgate. Before the amalgamation of the two towns, Hartlepool Corporation had blue buses, while West Hartlepool had red ones. When Richardsons and Grays knocked off for the day, the traffic (mainly bicycles) was so great at Throston Bridge and Middleton Road junctions that policemen were required to be on point duty to control the traffic.

Sandwell Gate

The word 'iconic' is vastly overused today to the point that is often utterly meaningless (a bit like 'nice'). However, if there was anything that could be called iconic in old Hartlepool then it is the Sandwell Gate. Here are two atmospheric photographs: one taken at the turn of the twentieth century, the other some 100 years later.

23

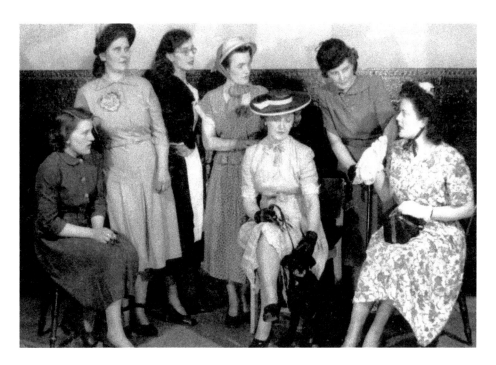

'A World Without Men' or The Wizard of Oz?

Whatever your choice in entertainment, these two photographs would seem to cover the whole spectrum. The older, more sedate, picture shows St Hilda's Amateur Dramatic Society presenting *World Without Men* at St Hilda's Hall in the early 1950s. The ladies are Joan Longmoor, Blanche Wanley, -?-, Mrs Hunter, Gladys Bradford, Betty Waller and Joyce Hastings. The newer photograph is Hartlepool Stage Society's dress rehearsal at Hartlepool Town Hall Theatre for *The Wizard of Oz* in May 2014.

The Cyclists' Lifeboat

A fascinating page from *The Graphic* of 14 December 1887 celebrating the launch of the Hartlepool lifeboat, as presented by the Cyclists of Great Britain. Spectators lined the harbour and some watched from packed steamers; some 6,000 'wheelmen' subscribed to the boat; it served until 1902. The Hartlepool lifeboat story began in 1802 at Castle Eden when, mindful of the great storm of 1785 when thirty-three vessels were wrecked or grounded between Hartlepool and Seaton Carew, it was decided that a lifeboat be built for the Port and Harbour of Hartlepool; the boat began service in 1803. By the 1850s, there were lifeboats housed at Sandwell Chare, the Old Pier and at North Sands, 2 miles north of the Heugh; the obligatory West Hartlepool Harbour & Railway Company boats were at Stranton beach near Newburn Bridge and in the West Harbour. Today's photograph is of the Trent Class lifeboat 14-12, the RNLB *Forward Birmingham* in Hartlepool Marina in November, 2013. She is now part of the Royal National Lifeboat Institution relief fleet.

Breeches Buoy Practice

In 1931, two boys getting a close-up of the lifeboat crews perfecting this time-honoured, life-saving device on Middleton Sands. The picture appeared in my *Lifeboat Stations of the North East*, proceeds of which go to the RNLI; it was originally published in George Colley's *The Sands of Time*. The contemporary photograph depicts training with life-saving technology of a very different kind. The scene was part of a Hartlepool RNLI Open Day in 2010: a rescue exercise with Hartlepool's own Trent Class lifeboat, the RNLB *Betty Huntbatch,* and a RAF Sea King Rescue helicopter.

Shifting Fish on the Fish Quay

Lol Richardson (on the left above) doing the hard work during an auction in the 1970s. Working the auctions, or 'reading the markets', at the quay to obtain the best price required skills and intuition as sharp as any found on the trading floors of city financial institutions. When the fish was sold and the tallies applied to the boxes, they were moved to the fish merchants where it was sorted and boxed according to destination in the UK. Lids were nailed down and destination tallies were affixed before the boxes were loaded on to the appropriate railway trucks. Before the introduction of filleting, fish were always despatched whole. The new picture is of the fishing boat *Carolyn* returning to Hartlepool.

Proud Fisherman and Predatory Gulls

Obviously a special occasion for these proud Hartlepool fishermen – if nothing else it was a very good day's catch. The gulls in the new picture are obviously expecting similar pickings as they follow a fishing boat into the harbour.

Blazing Sleepers

During and after: the lamp-post-melting fire at the George Horsely & Son timber yard around Cleveland Road in 1922 destroyed 300,000 railway sleepers and a creosote factory. The aftermath shows nearby rolling stock and houses that had been gutted during the conflagration.

Old Hartlepool by Night

Pilot's Pier Lighthouse and the war memorial in Redheugh Gardens are resplendent at night. The Winged Victory (or Triumphant Youth) memorial remembers the 240 'Citizens, Servicemen and Servicewomen of the Borough of Hartlepool who gave their lives in conflict and War during the years from 1919 to 1967'. Those who died during the 1914 bombardment are also remembered.

Chick Henderson (1912–44)

Chick Henderson was born Henderson Rowntree; he went to Galleys Field School; 'Chick' was simply his mother's nickname for him. He made his first recordings for Harry Leader in 1935 and in 1936 began singing for Joe Loss's radio orchestra, staying with him for five years. Henderson made over 250 recordings but, as with many big band singers, his name rarely appeared on the record label – only the orchestra was credited. In July 1939, he and Joe Loss recorded *Begin the Beguine*, which sold over a million copies; it was the only recording by a 1930s artist to achieve such sales. On 7 October 2009, Susan Wappat uploaded a video on YouTube with the following text: 'Everyone (including his wife) believed that the 1930s crooner Chick Henderson was killed by shrapnel from a British Ack-Ack gun during an air raid towards the end of WWII. Frank Wappat of the BBC has investigated and proved beyond any doubt that the story was fabricated by naval officials when a lone German bomber got through radar undetected and strafed the hotel where naval personnel were stationed. Chick was the only casualty. The full story won a Sony Award for Frank Wappat.' Wappat is also the author of *The Chick Henderson Story,* pictured here and available from enquiries@atkinsonprint.com in Hartlepool. Twenty years after Henderson's death, The Searchers came to town to top the bill at The Big Beat Show, which was held on Hartlepool Promenade. The programme came from the collection of Mike Watson, a member of The Corantos, who appeared on the bill that day.

Old and West Post Offices

The Old Hartlepool post office on the corner of Vollum's Chare, named after William Vollum, a mayor of Hartlepool. The mock Tudor building was the original library (looks like a former pub but it never was) to be replaced by the Carnegie Library in Northgate in 1904. The West Hartlepool General Post Office features in the colour photograph; it opened in 1900 in Whitby Street.

General Post Office. West Hartlepool.

Empire Day and the Tall Ships

The town's ability to draw a crowd is very much in evidence from these two photographs, marking spectacular events over a century apart. The 1908 celebrations for Empire Day (the annual observance of the birthday of Queen Victoria) are enjoyed by tens of thousands of residents and visitors, many dressed up or in uniform for the occasion. In 2010, Hartlepool was chosen to host the second and final leg of the 2010 Tall Ships Race – just look at the crowds here, repeated over four days that summer.

THE BATHING POOL, HARTLEPOOL.

The Swimming Pool and the Sea

The sea put paid to the open-air swimming pool during the great storm of January 1953. Here it is again in an unusual shot through Sandwell Gate looking over to Pilot's Pier Lighthouse. The white, square pyramidal wooden tower lighthouse was built in 1836 and is still operational: it flashes every three seconds, white over entrance channel, or otherwise green, as can be seen here.

CHAPTER 2

West Hartlepool

The Town Hall Theatre

The lights go up on the 404-seater Victorian Gothic theatre in Raby Road, a wonderful conversion of the town hall built in 1896. Here it is brilliantly lit at night, showing off its Gothic splendour to great effect. The earlier shot depicts contractors setting up for a trade exhibition in the theatre. The pictures on the previous page show pre-amalgamation signage for the town on the A19 and the Marina at dusk with the rigging of *Trincomalee* silhouetted on the left and St Oswald's church in the centre. The *Trincomalee* is one of only two surviving British frigates of the time – her sister ship, HMS *Unicorn,* is also a museum ship, berthed in Dundee. The *Trincomalee* was built in Bombay from teak, due to a shortage of oak in Britain caused by shipbuilding frenzy for the Napoleonic Wars. It is named after the victorious 1782 Battle of Trincomalee against the French and cost £23,000. *Trincomalee* was launched on 12 October 1817 and then sailed to Portsmouth Dockyard on a journey costing £6,600.

Joe Brown, a Co-author and Two Footballers

Above, Hartlepool United footballers Cliff Wright and the late Terry Bell, together with pop singer Joe Brown and co-author Stan Laundon, in 1967. The photograph, courtesy of *The Hartlepool Mail*, was taken in Kildale Grove, Seaton Carew. Joe was appearing in cabaret at The Club Fiesta in Stockton and was staying at Stan's house at the time. Bell and Wright were, of course, part of that famous team who won promotion to the then Third Division in the 1967/68 season. Terry played 123 games for Pools, scoring thirty-eight goals. The colour picture below shows on-tour Joe Brown with Stan Laundon outside the Forum Theatre, Billingham in 2009.

The Docks, Hartlepool.

Old Ships and Tall Ships
A 1930s picture of ships in Hartlepool harbour matched with a night shot of some of the tall ships in 2011.

The Home Front

The cover of this booklet published by Tees Archaeology in 2006 features an interesting selection of local Second World War pictures: local school gas mask practice; (middle from left) emerging from a West Hartlepool Anderson Shelter; the Home Guard marching through West Hartlepool; bomb damage in Church Street; (lower from left) Sgt G. Hatton, 4th Btn North Riding of Yorkshire Home Guard; a pillbox at Greatham & Auxiliary Fire Service next to a requisitioned Binns van. Copies are available at www.teesarchaeology.com. Three people died in the bombing of Church Street in August 1940; the Edgar Phillips building next to the Yorkshire Penny Bank was destroyed (*see page 47*), as was the Clarence Hotel. More gas mask drill in the other picture in which the Local Defence Volunteers go through the paces.

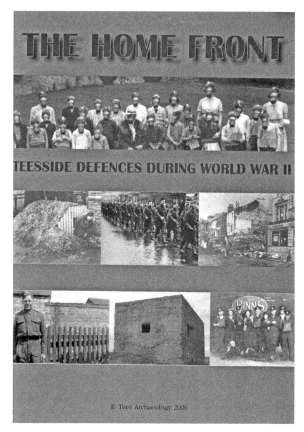

The Steelworks
A fine aerial view of the North Works with some of the workers there posing for the camera.
Spot the boss.

The Physics Lesson

A physics lesson in 1928 at Hartlepool Grammar School. Things were much the same when I was there forty years later in 1968. Note the ominous presence of two 'masters', and spot the cane: I can't, but it's bound to be there somewhere. Hartlepool Sixth Form College now occupies the site: the modern photograph shows the physics laboratory there in 2014. LHC (on the poster on the right) is CERN's Large Hadron Collider: 'the work of 10,000 men and women from across the globe, united in their quest to uncover the fundamental building blocks of our universe ... this immersive exhibition blends theatre, video and sound art with real artifacts from CERN, recreating a visit to the famous particle physics laboratory'; so says the website for the exhibition at The Science Museum. *The Independent*'s review hits the nail on the head: 'a bold endeavour to bring fundamental physics to the people ... in many ways it's better than the real thing [visiting CERN].'

Churchill Comes To Town

Smiling waitresses at the YMCA at No. 39 Whitby Street during the First World War, with happy looking uniformed customers. On 31 July 1940, Winston Churchill, soon after becoming Prime Minister, arrived in the towns on a morale-boosting visit inspecting coastal defences – the Hartlepools were considered possible invasion points for the Germans. The famous photograph that was taken of him wielding an American 1928 Tommy Gun (or Thompson SMG), and smoking a cigar, was used for propaganda by both sides. The British 'photoshopped' out some of the soldiers and officials in the background to make Churchill look more statesmanlike; the Germans, on the other hand, adapted the image to present Churchill as an American gangster and murderer. To Nazi propaganda minister Goebbels this was a gift: he used it extensively in Europe and in air drops over the UK during the Battle of Britain with the text in English 'WANTED', and at the bottom, 'for incitement to MURDER'. The reverse reads: 'This gangster, who you see in his element in the picture, incites you by his example to participate in a form of warfare in which women, children and ordinary citizens shall take the leading parts. This absolutely criminal form of warfare which is forbidden by the Hague Convention will be punished according to military law. Save at least your own families from the horrors of war!' A similar poster carried the word *Heckenschützen* (Sniper).

Church Street Cabin

The original signal box, which opened in 1880, outside the Railway Cabin at the bottom of Commercial Street. The signs reveal the local industry. They show timber and slate importers Joseph Griggs & Co. in Albert Terrace, later renamed Mainsforth Terrace, and timber merchants J. W. Baird & Co. The other photograph is of 'Flamboyant', the Class A1 Pacific steam locomotive 4-6-2 60153 at West Hartlepool station in 1951. The photograph was taken by the late Harry Henderson, supplied by his brother Bill Henderson.

The Greenside and Miss Great Britain

The sign apart, green is conspicuous by its absence. The pub used to be bathed in a lurid green light when Cameron's opened it in 1967, but sadly no more. Before being a pub the building was a private house which, in 1943, was converted into a probation hospital. The colour green, though, was never the company's main concern: their preoccupation was with a distinctly nautical theme, as satirically reported in *The Northern Daily Mail*: 'the nautical man o' war interior comes as a rollicking surprise ... [the] ingeniously converted ship's wheel chandelier and daylight roof do prepare one a little for the novel effect of the huge richly carpeted Chart Room ... the amber-lit bar, with its sky-blue, seagulled backing and collection of villainous cut-throat pirate drawings.' Lethal-looking pistols and full-size hammocks completed the paraphernalia. The other picture is of the 1980 Miss Greenside competition; Lesley Anne Musgrave is the lady on the right, later to be voted Miss Great Britain in 1986; the other two remain unidentified.

Birks' Cafe & Station Hotel

In 1911, Hugh Hallifield Birks, son of Edwin Birks, the founder of Hartlepool café and grocery shop chain Birks Bros, married Emily Douglas Lamb, daughter of Henry Lamb, founder of jeweller's and clockmaker's H. Lamb, which still trades in York Road. In Birks', there was a billiards room in the basement – for gentlemen only.

West Hartlepool VADs

Voluntary Aid Detachments were the county branches of the British Red Cross Society, trained in first aid and nursing. They were set up from 1909 and within six months numbered 6,000 volunteers, mainly middle class women anxious to do their bit. Their work included the administration of, and the provision of nursing care in convalescent homes and auxiliary hospitals. In 1914, qualified nurses joined them. They worked in kitchens, offices, drove ambulances and became civil defence and welfare officers. West Hartlepool was the first VAD detachment in the north-east, set up by Dr H. W. M. Strover in 1911. To cater for the local garrison, a twenty-five bed VAD hospital was established in the Masonic Hall in August 1914. Strover was the medical officer there; his wife, Margaret, was the commandant. During the 1914 bombardment, the hospital was described as a front line casualty clearing station, and was even hit by a German shell. The pictures show Margaret Strover and the staff and patients at the hospital after its later move to Normanhurst in Wooler Road.

Church Street

A bus and tram can be seen in this old 1920s picture, with a blind man tentatively crossing the road under the watchful eye of a fellow pedestrian. In fact, traffic was never a concern if the men walking towards the camera on the right are anything to go by – unlike the situation in the modern shot taken from the church tower. Church Street and the surrounding area suffered in the Second World War: on 27 August 1940 the Victoria Ground and the Greyhound Stadium were damaged and Scarborough Street was hit. The Yorkshire Penny Bank was flattened but carried on its business at No. 55 until rebuilding was complete. Next door, Edgar Phillips suffered the same fate and moved temporarily to John Street; two women and a man died there. The bombs caused parts of Church Street to sink, with some foundations subsiding up to 18 inches.

Air Raid Diary

The Luftwaffe attacks on Tees-side, 1940-1943

Bill Norman

Destruction in Hilda Street and Mainsforth Terrace

Hilda Street was close to Mainsforth Terrace and suffered considerable damage on the night of 30 August 1940. Two high-explosive bombs were dropped by a bomber on its way home: one scored a direct hit on a fish and chip shop on the corner of Mainsforth Terrace and Pilgrim Street. Unfortunately, eleven people were sheltering in the shop's cellar – nine were killed, the oldest of whom was Elizabeth Sarah Tarran (twenty-six); the youngest, William Tarran, was aged nine months. The other bomb exploded in Hilda Street, demolishing nineteen houses and damaging a further 120. Bill Norman's *Air Raid Diary* recounts in fascinating detail the Luftwaffe attacks on the Hartlepools and the surrounding area, complete with poignant casualty listings for each raid. It can be obtained from the author at www.billnorman.co.uk. (*Photographs courtesy of* The Northern Echo)

Queuing for Coke

Smiling for the camera, at least, this queue of women in the early 1930s are hopeful that they will be able to get some coke from the gasworks in Middleton Road to heat their homes. Never throw away your pram ... Meanwhile, at No. 3 Lambton Street, just off Lynn Street, Miss Frances Costede and her staff get ready for a day's work.

'The Flying Scotsman'

The A3 4-6-2 4472 (60103) 'Flying Scotsman' leaving Hartlepool. She was the last steam engine to be watered and bunkered at the sheds in Mainsforth Terrace before they finally closed. The modern picture shows a King's Cross to Sunderland train arriving at Hartlepool station – and about to run over our photographer!

Hartlepool Tourism
Some vibrant tourist advertising on Hartlepool railway station, focusing on the Tall Ships race.

Richardson's Coaches

What looks like a wedding group outside the Richardson's coach depot in Oxford Road in the 1940s. The coach is a Rio, an American make and the first with pneumatic tyres. The modern picture shows part of the Richardson's fleet in 2014.

The Circus and the Tall Ships Come to Town

Above we see elephants and camels processing along Wordsworth Avenue; below we have the happy crowds enjoying themselves at the 2010 Tall Ships event at the Marina.

WAR MEMORIAL AND VICTORIA ROAD, WEST HARTLEPOOL.

The War Memorial

The war memorial in Victoria Road. Apart from the fallen from West Hartlepool, there were substantial civilian casualties due to bombing raids. According to the official report by Sir Arthur Lambert, the North Regional Commissioner, there were seventy fatalities, sixty-six seriously injured and one hundred and sixty-one with lesser injuries. On the night of 19/20 June 1940 West Hartlepool suffered its first air-raid. Two people were killed; one of them was John Punton, an air raid warden who was the first full-time civil defence worker to die in a raid. There were forty-three air raids on the Hartlepools between June 1940 and March 1943; of the seventy deaths, forty-eight were at West Hartlepool (fourteen men, seventeen women and seventeen children); twenty-two were at Hartlepool (six men, twelve women and four children). West Hartlepool had 480 warnings but only thirty-six raids in which bombs were dropped, in which 5,745 buildings were damaged or destroyed. Hartlepool had seven raids in which 1,771 buildings were damaged or destroyed.

The Travellers Rest For Your Orchestral Entertainment

Cameron's sparkling ales have been replaced with fare courtesy of the Flaming Grill Pub Co. The pub was built in 1840 by a William Wass, who ran it as landlord; Cameron's took it on in 1895. In 1936, the brewery decided to demolish the building and replace it with a new one as 'a roadhouse of the type which has in the past few years become very popular in the South of England', according to *The Mail* in December 1936. It was not to be a pub in the traditional sense but 'a social centre where residents of the town, and visiting motorists may spend a pleasant evening listening to an orchestra, and enjoying an occasional dance, with all the facilities of a modern restaurant and hotel ... an atmosphere of an old English country home.' Recognise it?

The ABC Forum, Outside

The ABC Cinema in Raby Road directly opposite the police station opened as The Forum in 1937 and in 1958 became the ABC. Before it closed in 1983 it was the Fairworld Cinema. The 1937 photograph comes courtesy *Old Cinema Photographs* by Dusashenka. The film showing at the time was *This'll Make You Whistle* a 1936 British musical comedy starring Jack Buchanan. The second photograph is of The Empire in Lynn Street – a beautiful Renaissance-style theatre, which opened in 1909 and was tragically demolished in 1975 in a breathtaking act of civic vandalism. Max Bygraves, Pat Phoenix and Morecambe and Wise trod the boards here in the 1950s.

Lynn St. West Hartlepool, Showing Empire.

The ABC Forum, Inside

Two shots of the interior: the upper is of the elegant reception and foyer. The wall poster, on the extreme right, advertises the 1936 film *Juggernaut*, a thriller starring Boris Karloff. The lower shows the upper floor; coming soon is the 1936 *The Road To Glory* starring Fredric March. Thanks again to Dusashenka's *Old Cinema Photographs*.

Herring the Horse Slaughterer
The badge and the cart James Herring and his son used in their horse slaughtering business at No. 95 Oxford Road around 1935 are perfectly preserved in the Museum of Hartlepool. What sounds like a close relative was Harry Herring, who had business connections with Beeline coaches in Oxford Road and farming interests in Carlisle and Hartlepool, at the 'The Riding School' at Southbeck farm off Catcote Road. The old picture is a postcard sent to a Mr P. Craman of Darlington advising him that his horse died of 'T.B. on the lungs'.

The Port of Hartlepool
This stunning 1909 North Eastern Railway poster graphically depicts the situation of the port of Hartlepool and West Hartlepool, and their connections to the rail network.

Stranton

The wedding in the older picture took place in 1951 in Stranton church between Sgt Eric Wright Chrystal and Ruby Richardson. Others in the photograph are, from left to right, Joe Richardson (of the bus company family), Florence Priest (the bride's aunt and daughter-in-law of Fred Priest, England footballer and player coach of Hartlepools United, see page 75), Andrew McCreadie in kilt, Muriel (the groom's sister) and Tom McCreadie.

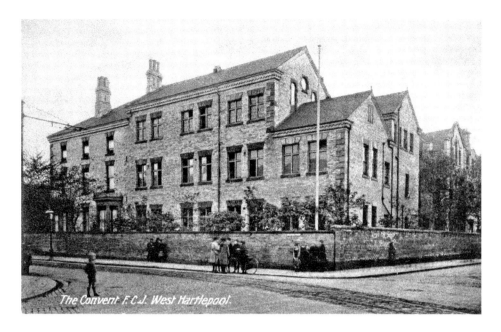

The Convent F.C.J. West Hartlepool.

The FCJ Convent

The order of nuns was the Faithful Companions of Jesus in Grange Road. This school opened in 1885, taking in girls from Hartlepool and South East Durham. The nuns had moved from St Hilda's convent in Redcar to Grange Road, where the address was, confusingly, 'Avon Villa', Victoria Road. In 1973, the last girls were transferred to English Martyrs; in 1976, the community moved to Hutton Avenue while the impressive school building was demolished in 1978. The order had arrived in London in 1830 under the aegis of Marie Madeleine d'Houet, the Foundress, and Julie Guillemet. They soon set up a number of convents and proceeded to educate for the next 150 years – the provision of education, especially for the young and poor, was the enduring hallmark and mission of the order.

Grange Road.   West Hartlepool.

Grange Road

A picture of Grange Road in the late 1920s, with a trolleybus on the way and St Paul's church on the left, and in the modern photograph. The church opened in 1885. The trolleybus system commenced on 28 February 1924, replacing the West Hartlepool part of the Hartlepool Electric Tramways. The first of the West Hartlepool tramways to be closed was the Foggy Furze line on 4 October 1923. The Ward Jackson Park tramway was next, in November 1925. The system had a fleet of forty-eight trolleybuses, with a maximum of thirty-one in service at any one time. None of them has survived.

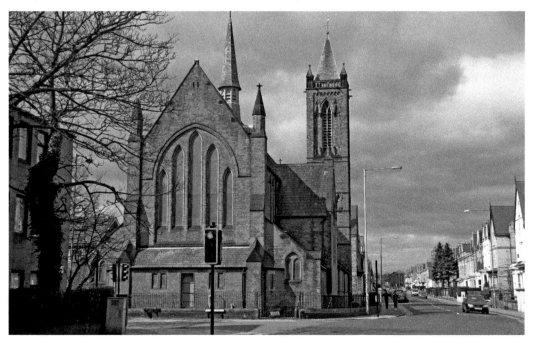

The DLI and *Whisky Galore*

'D' company of the 19th battalion of the
Durham Light Infantry (Bantams) returning to
their billet in West Hartlepool, the old
Co-op on the corner of Park Road and
Stockton Street. To qualify for the Bantams,
potential recruits had to be between 5 feet
and 5 feet 3 inches tall. During the First
World War, the battalion saw action on the
Somme and at Ypres, Albert and Courtrai.
Pte Theophilus Jones, of the 18th Btn DLI,
has the unfortunate distinction of being the
first soldier to die in action on British soil for
nearly two centuries and the first soldier to be
killed on British soil during the war. He was
the son of Mrs L. Jones, of No. 44 Ashgrove
Avenue, West Hartlepool. His brother, Alfred,
from the same battalion, was also killed.
Compton Mackenzie was the author of over
ninety books, some of which have been turned
into successful films. He was born in West
Hartlepool in 1883 during a stop-over made
by his actor parents while on tour. *Whisky
Galore* (1947) tells the story of how, during the
Second World War, the SS *Cabinet Minister* is
wrecked off Great Todday with 50,000 cases
of whisky on board; the thirsty islanders
salvage several hundred cases before the ship
sinks and are pursued by the officious English
Home Guard Captain Paul Waggett.

COMPTON MACKENZIE

WHISKY GALORE

PENGUIN BOOKS 3/6

Victoria Road

Some macabre Hartlepool happenings: in July 1727, William Stephenson, a grocer from Northallerton, was hanged at Durham for the murder of Mary Farding, who he had thrown into the sea at Hartlepool near The Maiden's Bower. In 1762, several whales were driven ashore by a severe storm; in 1778, Susan Corner, widow, was buried age 106. In 1790, a human body, complete and fully dressed, was discovered in a coffin – it turned to dust on exposure to the air, except for the soles of the corpse's boots, which 'were cut up and distributed amongst the curious of the town'. In 1799, several meteors were seen by Hartlepool fishermen at around 5 a.m. and continued falling from the sky until dawn. Sometimes the sky looked as though it was displaying a luminous serpent exploding and falling in a shower of fire.

Ward Jackson Park

A fine day out in the park – in Edwardian times and today. The charity dispensed by Henry Smith, and described on page 14, was not for everyone, and had some notable exclusions; they included 'any person who should be given to excessive drinking, whoremongers, common swearers, pilferers … any person disobedient to those whose servants they should have been, vagrant persons, [anyone] who should refuse to work'. That must have narrowed it down quite considerably.

Burn Valley Gardens, West Hartlepool.

Burn Valley Gardens

Tourism in (Old Hartlepool) made a hesitant start in 1844, but there was (gas) light at the end of the tunnel: 'in the Bathing season the town is full of company but the accommodation in the way of lodgings and baths is bad ... gas has lately been introduced ... and at night a view of the town from any of the surrounding heights is truly enchanting. The Docks and Railway being well bespangled with jets of spangled lights which are placed at different points as beacons to the mariner add splendour to the scene.' The 'authority' adds that a supply of 'good clear soft water' would help, for at at the time it was brought in by cart and sold by the pail.

Egbert the Tank and the Submarine Tram

A tram was disguised as a German U-Boat outside what looks like the Raglan Hotel in Tower Street; the aim was to boost the war effort or enlist. A tank was enlisted in October 1917 to help West Hartlepool sell its share of national war bonds. The following February, *Nelson* rumbled up, performed some manoeuvres on the Armoury Field before taking up position in front of the Municipal Buildings for Tank Week. During the various events (which included the Picturedrome, an open-air cinema) local soldier Private Charles Burton was presented with the Military Medal for his valour in tending to wounded men at Passchendaele after he himself had been gassed. West Hartlepool's efforts were not to go unrewarded: *Egbert* was presented to the town, standing sentinel on Stranton Garth from April 1919. A massive £2,367,333 was raised. Ironically, *Egbert* was later melted down, quite probably to help produce tanks in the Second World War.

Foggy Furze

It's all go in Foggy Furze. The two children in the trolleybus have got the best seats while the *Dog World Annual* for 1949 extols Fred Gent's breeding expertise in his kennels in Oxford Street, or at least that of his Cairn Terriers and Bedlingtons. The night of 19 August 1940 was one of the worst of the war for West Hartlepool: twenty-two people died when a parachute mine fell on Elwick Road and Houghton Street – the eldest fatality was eighty-nine-year-old Emily Edmundson, the youngest two year old Eric Littlefair who perished with four other members of his family. At No. 23 Elwick Road Alex and Nellia Tomson were in bed when the mine exploded; Alex exhibited exceptional strength when he, a gymnast and weight lifter, caught a heavy beam that was about to fall on Nellia, his wife. He kept it off her for two hours; sadly Nellia later died.

Strike a Light at the Match Factory

NEMCO (North of England Match Co.) had its own conflagration to deal with in 1954 when their factory was totally destroyed, much to the fascination of the crowds that poured into Church Street to watch, some even buying platform tickets at the station to get a closer look. The other photograph shows attempts to extinguish the fire from Swainson Dock.

The College of Further Education

The fine building that is the College of Further Education is the latest in a long line of educational and training establishments on the site going back to 1897. Resources include an aircraft hangar housing two ex-RAF Jet Provost T5s, a Westland Gazelle Helicopter and a Rolls-Royce airliner engine; a sports science laboratory. The jet in the gardens is an ex-RAF Jet Provost T5 XW405; it arrived in June 2012 and was fully stripped, repainted and rebuilt by students and staff. It retains the red, white and grey colours of the RAF Flight Training School from the late 1980s.

Bomb Damage and a Messerschmitt

Two pictures which characterise the impact of the Second World War on West Hartlepool. One shows bomb damage inflicted on Brenda Road (uncomfortably close to the South Durham Iron & Steelworks) on 26 August 1940. The other picture is of a captured German Messerschmitt Bf109 shot down over Kent in late 1940 by a Spitfire from 92 Squadron. It was flown by Gefr. Hubert Rungen and crashed at Cuckold Coombe near Ashford. Here it is shown on the Bull Field on a tour of England, which also included the Guildhall in London and Durham.

The Demise of Sea-Coal Hawking

A fascinating picture of sea-coal hawkers, plying their trade in 1912. Sea-coaling has been an integral part of life in Hartlepool since the seventh century: the tides erode coal from the sea bed, which is then washed up on the beach. A hawker can harvest more than a tonne of coal every day, which is then sold on to power plants. A full-page article entitled 'Boys from the Black Stuff', published on 9 April 2001 in *The Guardian*, described the Hartlepool sea-coaler's life; here is a short extract: 'No day is the same for the sea-coalers. They work the tides, and consequently find themselves heading for the foreshore at any and every hour of the 24. Seven days a week. Theirs is the rota of the moon ... each seacoaler has had to learn to speak the language of the sea as fluently as any fisherman.' In October 2013, the council took steps to end the trade for the nineteen or so hawkers who still worked the beaches at Seaton Carew. Industry of an entirely different sort is shown in the second photograph: here ship cleaners are hard at work in Middleton Dry Dock in 1908 while the foreman looks on, with Richardsons Westgarth in the background.

Richardson's Charabanc and Bee Line

All set for a good day out to somewhere, this gives a fascinating glimpse of road transport around 1920. Richardson's still trades today in Oxford Road, as does rivals Bee Line; one of their days out to East Row, Sandsend, near Whitby, is shown in the other photograph. At the end of the Second World War, West Hartlepool replaced its trolleybuses and with motorbuses and a joint operation of the service connecting West Hartlepool and Hartlepool commenced. Hartlepool had to provide half of the buses, which caused something of a problem since they had no buses. An agreement was reached with the United Counties Omnibus Company, who would operate the four buses needed, but this was short-lived. A similar agreement was reached with Bee Line Roadways who ran the service on Hartlepool Corporation's behalf from August 1953. The Hartlepool Corporation bus fleet comprised four ex-London Transport Bristol's liveried in blue and cream, and was garaged at the Bee Line depot with any vehicle shortages being made good from Bee Line's own fleet.

Hartlepools Cup Fever and the Munitionettes

This was the score at the October 1908 FA Cup tie between the two local teams at the Victoria Ground; it was the first game United played in the FA Cup, although the amateurs of West Hartlepool had done it all many times before. United's captain was Fred Priest; attendance was a respectable 7,000. Smith, with arm raised, is the scorer of United's second goal. United went out in the next round, beaten at home 2-1 in a replay by South Bank. Below we have a rare picture of the Oxford Street William Brown Sawmill Girls' football team, finalists in the Munitionette Cup final 1918/19. By today's standards, women's football was extraordinarily popular, especially among industry, with many teams formed from munitions workers (Munitionettes) around the country during the First World War. They were not just casual kickabouts, but proper matches played at prestigious venues, such as St James's Park and Ayresome Park. For more teams visit www.donmouth.co.uk/womens_football/images – 'the most extensive collection of research into the early history of women's football'.

Fred Priest

Alfred Ernest (Fred) Priest was the first manager and captain of Hartlepools Utd from 1908 to 1912. Previously, he had played for England in 1900 and Sheffield United (as a left winger or inside left); he was also assistant coach at Middlesbrough. At Sheffield he had won League Championship and Cup winners' medals; in 1897/98 when 'The Cutlers' won the League title, Fred was leading goalscorer. Fred's three-year contract at Hartlepool showed him to have been paid £3 a week; even allowing for inflation Wayne Rooney's £300,000 a week seems a little generous. Alfred's son, Eric Priest, carried on the footballing tradition when he became manager of Richardsons Westgarth; he was also landlord of The Malt and Hops in Albert Street in the 1950s – it closed in 1959. Eric's brother, Jackie, was landlord of The Dun Cow Inn on the corner of Northgate and Francis Street in 1950.

Hartlepools Utd and the Zeppelins

The day of 27 November 1916 is memorable in the history of Hartlepool United; it was on that day during the First World War that two German Zeppelins, pursued by a Royal Flying Corps pilot, offloaded their bombs onto the Victoria Ground. The main stand was demolished. The club pursued a long-running claim for £2,500 against the German Government as war reparation: all the club got in reply was the Second World War, during which the ground narrowly escaped further destruction. The pictures show Victoria Park today, with all stands intact, and a Zeppelin from 1916. There were fifty-two Zeppelin raids on Britain during the war, claiming the lives of more than 500 people. At York on 2 May 1916, eighteen bombs were dropped on the city, killing nine and injuring forty more. Details of this raid and two others in 1916 were suppressed until 1956. A doctor at the local Retreat psychiatric hospital circulated a letter on worrying levels of 'Zeppelinophobia' among the populace.

The End of the Trolleybus

The end of the trolleybus came in 1953. The pictures show a trolleybus en route to Foggy Furze being overtaken by a bus, and council workmen taking down the overhead wires in Grange Road. The First World War had an impact on West Hartlepool Corporation Tramways' recruitment policy. With many men away at the Front, women were called up to step in: by March 1916, twenty-eight out of thirty-three conductors were women; in 1917 there were also five women drivers with thirteen drivers by March 1918. Recruitment policy had changed again by 1921 when all the women were replaced by men. Not much equal opportunity then.

Upper and Lower Church Street

Looking up and down Church Street – the one, a fine old postcard from 1914 with a trolleybus in the distance, the other a 1960s photograph. The Shades Hotel can just be seen below to the right of the double-decker bus; The Royal Hotel is the last building on the left. The Shades retains its marvellous façade. It was opened in 1856 by a Robert Baxter,s a whisky blender and wine and spirit merchant. 'Shades' was a slang nineteenth-century term for beer vaults. Cameron's bought the pub in 1895. The Royal opened in 1844 and was owned by North Eastern Railways until it was sold to Vaux.

Cameron's

Cameron's chimney with the brewery smoking away, and the old Co-op building with Stranton church visible between the two; it was taken from Christ Church tower. An attractive Cameron's poster from the early twentieth century; it shows various parts of the brewery and Cameron's pubs.

Perry's

Two photographs of Perry's, the electrical and television store, in Victoria Road – one from the early 1970s, the other (the colour one) from April 1997. The history of Perry's begins in Lower Church Street when, in 1912, Captain Percival Forest Perry, a nautical optician, bought No. 11 for £1,050. The façade was refashioned to include the prow of a ship protruding from the first floor; the office was designed to replicate a ship's bridge. Perry then established the West Hartlepool Academy – in effect a school of wireless telegraphy for merchant seamen. The First World War kept Perry busy, but by 1933 the Academy had closed. Nevertheless, he continued trading in various ships' instruments, although the real demand was for wireless sets: receivers branded Perriphones 3 and 4 were manufactured on site under a George Cormack. The firm also produced wirelesses for home construction. Perry died in 1934 but Cormack presided over a period of expansion until the outbreak of the Second World War, when most of the staff where called up, except Cormack who was in a reserved occupation maintaining compasses for the Royal and Merchant Navies. After the war, the focus moved towards radio and television; Perry's sold the premises in 1959 for £1,000 to a Mr Ho Hong, who established a Chinese restaurant there. They moved to Victoria Road, where they thrived until 2012, when the business closed.

CHAPTER 3

Around Hartlepool

The Seaton High Light

The older photograph was taken around 1982 at its original site in the grounds of Bachelor Robinson, Windermere Road, in Longhill. The stunning new picture shows it as it is today: re-erected stone by stone on Jackson's Landing in the Marina in 1997, dedicated to those who lost their lives at sea. Acting under increasing commercial pressure from the docks at West Hartlepool the Tees Navigation Co. was forced to improve access to the River Tees: the High Light was opened in 1839, one of two navigation light towers at Seaton to guide ships. The Low Light was at the end of Queen Street, near the Staincliffe. The Low Light was a 70-foot-tall hexagonal tower and exhibited a fixed red light. The High Light is a 70-foot-tall Tuscan column, which exhibited a fixed white light. The High Light became obscured by the works of the West Hartlepool Steel & Iron Co. and was decommissioned by the Tees Conservancy Commissioners in 1892.

New Bus Station, Seaton Carew.

Seaton Carew Bus Station

A wonderful pair of pictures of this fine Art Deco Grade II listed bus station, which opened in 1938. In November 1916, during the First World War, four Zeppelins attacked Hartlepool: one, the L34, was caught in a searchlight to the west of Hartlepool and Lieutenant Ian Vernon Pyott, a pilot with 36 Squadron based at Seaton Carew, pursued the Zeppelin for 5 miles, intermittently firing at his prey. The L34 caught fire and plummeted into Tees Bay with the loss of all crew.

Dove-Cote Ice Creams, Seaton Carew
The Lollie Van and the Dove-Cote diploma ice cream van with owner Ken Tyzack and employee Stan Prestedge in the late 1950s. Dove-Cote ice cream was made at the rear of Ken's amusement arcade on the sea front in Seaton Carew.

What the Butler Saw in Seaton Carew...

Ice cream was not the only feather in Ken Tyzack's cap. Here is a wonderful shot of the peep show in the amusement arcade. The 'customer' is certainly spoilt for choice. The other picture shows another of Ken Tyzack's contributions to the attractions at Seaton.

Seaton from North Gare

An unusual shot of Seaton taken from North Gare, showing it at its best. Seaton had to deal with Zeppelins in the First World War; in the Second World War it was the Luftwaffe's bombers; for example, on 6 January 1942 there were daylight machine-gun and bombing attacks at Seaton Carew; two high-explosive bombs were dropped on the Zinc Works; the works office was demolished, the distillation plant and a number of houses nearby were damaged and three people were injured. The other picture shows Seaton as it was in the 1950s – Britain's answer to Coney Island – but sadly it is no more.

Seaton's Industrial Past

A shot of the steelworks bridge in 1982 just north of Seaton. The steelworks were an obvious target for the Luftwaffe during the war: on 24/25 August 1940, thirteen high-explosive bombs fell, causing considerable damage to the works: a fifty-six-year-old man was killed. The other picture is another view of the bus station in the 1950s.

Old Elwick

Two evocative scenes of Elwick from the early twentieth century, highlighting the rural character of the village. Pictured are the old forge and a typical farming scene. The forge was on the corner of The Green and the west side of The Ghyll.

Haymaking at Dalton Piercy

Haymakers from Elwick pause for their dinner break and a cup of tea in the early 1900s. On 2 March 1963, the journalist and historian described in *The Northern Daily Mail* what he believed to be an accurate description of Elwick in 1879: 'in those days the road from West Hartlepool was more than four miles long, and rough cart-track most of the way ... a few steps down a small incline brought you to a white gate, at the top of the picturesque village, all ...whitewashed cottages and red-tiled roofs ... on The Green could be found the celebrated Elwick geese and here the dogs, pigs and boys of the village spent much of their time. On the left was the smart redbrick Methodist Chapel and beyond that The Spotted Cow and the MacOrville.' The colour picture is one of the fine windows in the twelfth-century St Peter's church – this one showing St George and St Lucy. St Lucy was a martyr executed in AD 304 in Syracuse; she is the patron saint of the blind.

Christ † Church,

West Hartlepool.

CLERGY.

Canon Macdonald, Rural Dean,
The Vicarage.
Rev. John Todd, B.A.,
12, Scarborough Street.

Wardens.

Mr. J. Sanderson, "Cliveden."
Mr. T. H. Todd, 19, Farndale
Terrace, Thornton Street.

Organist.

Mr R. Fawcett.

Verger : Mr. Fulcher,
32, South Road.

Parish Magazine.

Elwick Hall Church

Rector :
Rev. H. Williamson, M.A.

Wardens :
Mr. Geo Angus,
Middle Stotfod,
Mr. F. Bacon,
Elwick

Verger :
Mr. App. Harwood,
Church Side.

Hart Church :

Vicar :
Rev. J. C. Douglas, M.A.

Wardens :
Mr J. E. Sherwood
Mr. Thos. Darling.

Organist :
Miss Norah Douglas.

Verger :

St. Peter's, Elwick Hall.

St. Mary Magdalen, Hart.

December, 1920.

Price : Twopence.

The Churches of Elwick, Hart and West Hartlepool

The cover of the December 1920 *Parish Magazine,* showing these three churches. The modern photograph is of Saint Mary Magdalene in Hart. The first evidence of a place of worship here dates back to a wooden church in AD 675; it was later replaced by a stone building with a chancel and nave. During Norman times, St Mary Magdalene was part of the de Brus family estates. Somewhat later, nets were thrown over the ivy, which grew on the church to catch the sparrows, which were then made into sparrow pies.

Almshouses of the Hospital of God

These fascinating old photographs show Whitehouse Farm and the old Co-op at Greatham. The farm is now Whitehouse Farm Almshouses, a conversion of the dilapidated farm building completed in September 2011 by the Hospital of God comprising four two-bedroom apartments. The Hospital of God has sixty-five almshouses in Greatham, some are conversions as new as Whitehouse Farm, and others are more than 200 years old; all are modified to provide the highest standards for the residents. The Co-op incorporated a butchers at the far end; the white house on the left was the post office and dairy, demolished in 1976.

Greatham Feast, 1921

The Greatham Feast has been held annually for some 550 years and still attracts crowds. The Sheaf Thrower, by Michael Disley, was erected in 19 June 1995 and celebrates one of the original events at the feast. William Page, in his *History of the County of Durham Vol. 3* from 1928 describes the feast as follows: 'A yearly "feast" is held, however, on St John Baptist's Day (24 June), and is known as "Greatham Midsummer".'

Greatham and Wolviston

Two evocative pictures of the old post office at Greatham from the 1950s and St Peter's church in Wolviston. It was built in 1876 to replace a medieval chapel, and is typical of late Victorian brick-built village churches. Legend has it that Wolviston was named after the wolves in the area; however, it derives from Wulfestun (or Wulf's estate) or from a local Saxon landowner called Wolvis.

GREETINGS
from
Blackhall Colliery.
2368

Blackhall and Michael Caine

Blackhall's colliery closed in 1981. Blackhall beach is, of course, famous for its appearance in the 1971 film *Get Carter* where, at the end, Michael Caine is involved in a chase across a sea-coa-covered beach. The modern image shows the Miner's Wheel at Blackhall commemorating all those who worked, and those who died working, at Blackhall pit. Blackhall Rocks was, in the mid-nineteenth century, a holiday resort, due largely to the hotel up on the cliffs; a railway line and station was established to bring holidaymakers from Sunderland and Hartlepool in. It was closed in 1960, although the hotel survived until the 1970s when it was demolished.

DENE AND PADDLING POOL, CRIMDON

Crimdon

The railway viaducts at Crimdon and Dene Holme were built in 1905; Blackhall Rocks station opened for passenger trains and eight houses for railway workers were built. This marked the beginning of the association between Blackhall and the coal industry for the next seventy or so years. The sinking of the main shaft for mining coal began in 1909; the first coal came out in 1913. The revolutionary electric winding gear (which could excavate 18,000 tons a week) meant that there was no need for chimneys to spew out smoke and steam and no requirement for a slag heap because the waste was dumped into sea the by aerial ropeway; the pit was the most modern in Britain in 1916. Sadly, this industrial enlightenment was not reflected in the housing provision, which was shocking: initially, many families lived in huts and tents, even in the caves on the beach. A busy Crimdon Dene and a Blackhall colliery locomotive are in the pictures.

ACKNOWLEDGEMENTS

Without the help of a number of kind people this book would never have been published. Our thanks to the following for providing information and generously allowing us to reproduce their images, images that have enhanced the book no end: Eric Priest, for the information on Fred Priest and his contract; Jack Smurthwaite for the old Elwick pictures; George Colley for permission to use a number of images originally published in his *The Sands of Time* and in *Yesterday Once More*; Owen Corrigan for a number of pictures; Alan Grange; Martin Bingham; Doreen Richardson for the Richardson charabanc; David and Tot Richardson for the Richardson's Rio photograph; Mike Feather, West Hartlepool Grammar School Old Boys Association for the old physics class picture, www.whgsoba.org; Bill Henderson for the photographs of 'The Greenside' and other public houses; *The Flamboyant* at West Hartlepool station in 1951 was taken by the late Harry Henderson and supplied by his brother, Bill Henderson; Anita Roberts Tyzack for the Dove-Cote ice cream images, Seaton amusements, Town Hall Theatre and the elephant; Tony Pearson and Vic Smith for the old Hartlepool station photograph and details; Joan, Alan and Michael Gilfoyle for the photographs of Perry's; Ian Malcolmson for the DLI Regiment photograph; the blue bus under Throston Bridge comes courtesy of J. Graham Deacon; Carole Horseman, Acting Principal, Hartlepool Sixth Form College, kindly supplied the photograph of the college physics laboratory; thanks to Diane Marlborough, Reference & Information Manager, Hartlepool Central Library and Rachel Grahame, Tees Archaeology, for permission to reproduce the cover of *The Home Front: Teesside Defences During The Second World War*; Joy Yates, editor of *The Hartlepool Mail*, for permission to use the Joe Brown photograph originally published in *The Mail* – hundreds of fascinating images of the town are at www.hartlepoolmail. co.uk; Jacki Winstanley, Beamish People's Collection, kindly gave permission for the Cameron's advertisement and the U-Boat on page 67 to be used: www.beamish.org.uk/collections/ a fantastic archive; Peter Barron, editor of *The Northern Echo* allowed us to use the bomb damage picture in Hilda Street and the cover of Bill Norman's book, *Air Raid Diary: The Luftwaffe Raids on Teesside*; thanks to Bill Norman for allowing us to quote some of his casualty lists from the book; Mike Watson for The 'Searchers' programme; Roger Cornfoot for permission to use the Blackhall colliery locos picture; Gary Kester, Hartlepool College of Further Education, for details on the ex-RAF Jet Provost. More intriguing details on the Second World War bombing raids on the Hartlepools can be found at the obscurely named www.englandsnortheast.co.uk. Thanks for the ABC images to Dusashneka: www.flickr.com/photographs/oldcinemaphotographs. Patrick Brennan kindly gave permission to use the fascinating photographs of the Munitionettes and the West Hartlepool VADs; see his website for the history of women's football and other bits of North East history: www.donmouth.co.uk/womens_football/munitionettes.html.